HIS & HERS

Other books by Ric Masten

SPEAKING POEMS
Beacon Press

WHO'S WAVIN'
SUNFLOWERS
LET IT BE A DANCE

Other books by Billie Barbara Masten

OWING THE BEAST AND THE BAD GIRL
BILLIE BEETHOVAN

HIS & HERS a passage
through the middle-age crazies

by
the MASTENS

Ric & Billie Barbara

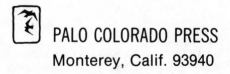

PALO COLORADO PRESS

Monterey, Calif. 93940

For our children Jeri
April
Stuart
& Ellen

Contents

BEYOND DIVORCE

THE TALK BACK

Including these poems

Preface

In the central section of this book you watch two separate voices ponder, protest, and celebrate the difficulties of female-male relationships. Ric faces you on the left, Billie Barbara on the right: you have the minister's eye view of the expectant man and woman. The dialogue is not perfectly synchronized. Ric's may be off in the clouds, or in Cleveland, while Billie Barbara is digging under the house or discovering herself through art. But more often than not the left and right-hand pages do speak to each other, or at least past each other to us. And that they often speak out of sync is an important part of what we hear.

The dialogue is continuous, kaleidoscopic, the divergence signaled by one type face for Ric and a different one for Billie Barbara. At two points the criss-crossing, independent voices merge, in the Annual Relationship Renewal Contract (1972) and the *warty frog* poem that ends the central section. Here there is unity, for the moment; but contract and poem were written by them jointly, and the type face itself declares this neutrality.

My few words here are also set in this third, neutral type face. Well I suppose I'm "neutral." but I am also thoroughly engaged. I'm here to represent the network of close friends the Mastens have developed throughout the country, particularly those amateur booking agents who create their yearly tours by lining up work: the more appearances we schedule, the longer we'll have Ric and Billie Barbara in our town, complicating and enlivening us and our friends. This is now the tenth year Ric's been on the road. It's the fourth for Billie Barbara. And so I and others have spent half a generation now watching them surge back and forth across the land, caught up in the foam of their surf. They've put themselves on display for us, acting out with art and emotion and humor and incredible energy the remarkable range of marital possibilities.

For a number of years it was Ric, solo. Each year he'd arrive for his week in Pittsburgh (or Kansas City, or Atlanta), staging the agonies and insights of the previous year for the frightening variety of audiences his ego demanded. ("But have you ever played a prison," he said recently to a poet friend; "how about a mental institution!") Each year I'd match up some of the vibrations in my own life with those Ric unpacked for us all with such clarity and insistence.

Billie Barbara was there too, of course, but unseen, the sea anchor to windward out on the mountain in California. And then came the year Ric was putting himself through one of the stormiest passages, the affair with a young admirer. Again, for many of us there were reverberations in our own lives, whether actual or fantasy. It wasn't really a surprise that Billie Barbara finally appeared in person the following year, trying out the water here in Pittsburgh, a particularly warm and receptive lake. There was a real edge to the Mastens' poems and songs that year, as Ric and Billie Barbara continued working furiously on overhauling their relationship, right there in our classrooms, churches, and kitchens.

So the Rorshach of the Masten art took on a new depth and variety, a whole new set of relevancies to our own lives. The next year Billie Barbara went on the road full-time with Ric, and the backwash in church and community groups was full of froth and foam. There isn't anyone in our culture who's uninterested in the birth/death and care/feeding of that perpetual invalid marriage. I knew that forcefully enough from my own life, but also because I found myself producing a record called "after the sunset again," the Masten marriage material as it stood in 1973. Following them around greater Pittsburgh, recording the talk-backs to use in the liner notes, I was struck by the dynamics of the response they provoked. That year we all suffered through our own divorces (fantasy, real, or symbolic) along with the Mastens.

x

Has it kept its edge? In some ways it's evened out, found more notes of celebration. But I think it still has its verve, its excitement, and I know from personal experience that it still packs a wallop, either in performance or on the page.

When they suggested I write the Preface for this latest incarnation of the marriage material, now far richer and more diverse and fertilized with the feedback of thousands of us over the years, my response was to wonder whether their marriage could weather the strain of putting the book together. Nothing's easy about joint authorship, about trying to achieve parity, especially when Ric had a substantial head start. It seems to me that they have managed to make the book balance. Female balances male, of course, and Billie Barbara's poetry has its own characteristic images and power that balance Ric's marvelous narrative line and insight.

Every time this ever-changing material is "caught" for a moment on plastic or paper, it achieves a false permanence. The plastic and paper may lie there unchanging, but the process that material lives, goes pulsating on: in the performance, where every new audience feeds in its response, and alters the experience for the next audience; in the Masten's own relationship, which keeps struggling and tugging at its seams; and in our own lives, as our new perspectives recreate the poems and songs for us every time we experience them.

Chris Rawson
Pittsburgh, Nov. 1977

Introduction

by
Billie Barbara

"Write the intro to the book."
"Shut up!" was my first reaction.
"Don't tell me what to do," still putting a father face on Ric and acting angry. I know now I do this to keep myself from doing things, even when it is something I want to do.

The poems here are some of the feelings we've had while being together twenty-five years; the first twenty in a traditional marriage, the last five contracting annually.

I feel excited writing this. Maybe the age has come when there is no elite, but many interested people sharing their stories — religion — the word made flesh. When experiences are put into symbols, language, shared not as right or wrong, the law, but ideas to spark others into creative fire, we wake up to our own power, creativity, and unique possibilities.

A classic couple, that's how I thought of us then, married during the fifties, trying to become mystically one person. I stayed in the house cleaning, learning to do wifery and mothering. Ric pursued his career as a song writer at night, making our living as a pressman in a small job shop by day while he learned to do husbandry and fathering. Impossible? I didn't think so, I just felt disappointed when he couldn't do them all equally well.

The excitement began to give way to boredom and routine. I felt at times utterly helpless, hopelessly dependent, not aware that I kept putting Ric into the father position. That's the way it was, is and shall always be. You have to suffer in this life. As a child you

*obey your father and mother. As a wife you must obey
your husband even if he doesn't want to be obeyed.*

*After twenty years of the above, we found ourselves in
a dead relationship, like the couple in a song Ric wrote,
entitled* robert and nancy. *He changed the names to
protect the innocent.*

> robert
> buried in the tribune with his coffee
> reading all about the day before
> nancy
> just across the table with her teacup
> studies what the tea leaves hold in store
>
> > and the now
> > the moment slips away
> > gone with its joy and sorrow
> > he was here yesterday
> > and she is coming tomorrow
>
> robert
> pictured in the yearbook — mr. football
> living in the dear departed past
> nancy
> nancy is prophetic — she's a pisces
> busy with the yarrow stalks she cast
>
> > and the now
> > the moment slips away
> > gone with its joy and sorrow
> > he was here yesterday
> > and she is coming tomorrow
>
> robert
> has a photograph of nancy in his office
> taken on the day that they were wed
> nancy
> goes to see a gypsy fortune teller
> wants to know what's lying up ahead
>
> > and the now
> > the moment slips away
> > gone with its joy and sorrow

he was here yesterday
and she is coming tomorrow

robert
puts away his toothbrush by the mirror
takes a look and sees his hair is gray
nancy
went to sleep in silence — what a pity
they never really lived at all did they?

they let the now
the moment slip away
gone are the joys and sorrow
but he was here yesterday
and she
was
coming tomorrow

we live together this way

HIS & HERS a passage
through the middle-age crazies

The Relationship

had a vision once
of a tower
here on the shoulder of this mountain
and went wild
with a hammer and a dream

but don't be overly impressed
with those
who build towers
any number of journeymen
carpenters
and stonemasons
can tell you how to do it

the building part is easy
it's the living in it
that comes hard

with some simple instruction
anyone can hang a door
but if you know the art
of oiling hinges

          teach me

HIS . . . a small quiet war

over the years my wife and i
have discovered two things
a man and a woman
should avoid doing together
that is
if they value their relationship
     laying rugs
       and carrying mattresses

and she's at it again
my wife
under the house digging

i can hear her down there
with my old rusty tools
picking and shoveling away
hollowing out a place
for her imagination to run wild in

she's been at it off and on
for two years now
running back and forth
with one shovel full of dirt at a time
throwing it into the yard
doing it the hard way
and i must admit
i'm always a bit surprised
and annoyed
when i see the size of the pile
she is making
but it's her project and she says
i'm not
and don't have to be involved

     still and all
     it has now become impossible
     for me to lie here comfortably
     listening to the ball game

HERS ... Little Bit

Mama could cut a chocolate
Into pieces enough for us
And the starving Chinese
So
I naturally thought
Everyone should share.
"Let me use your deodorant,
Some toothpaste,
A taste of your cheesecake please."

Sent away to boarding school
He hid the goodies his grandmother sent
From his roommates he learned
Not to share
Back home his mom
Gave him a whole Hershey
So naturally
He thought
Everyone should
Have one of their own

Whether this is female — male,
A parental tape, socio-economics
Or an old marriage game, who knows?

But in a bar
When he asks,
"Do you want a beer?"
And I say,
"No, but I'll have a little bit of yours."
     I know
     I go
     To far

HIS . . . on vacation

well — i bet we'd stop if it were you
who needed a service station!

not true — not true — says i to her boiling over
but driving through from dawn till dusk
grim as death — whipped along
by some primal hunting urge
to find the meat — kill it — and get it safely home

like all the desperate men i've seen
inching their machine along the california coast
i carry on
one eye on the calendar the other on the map
at the wheel but never feeling in the driver's seat

missing everything
except the double line
that hauls me through a Rand McNally nightmare
and leaves me sick with fear
hearing nothing but a queer sound in the engine
the obvious click — click — click click
that she puts down as my imagination
suggesting that perhaps the battery needs lubrication

when the time comes
i always take my leave like bitter medicine
watching the signs fly by
counting the miles and minutes off
praying that nothing goes wrong
till i'm back where i belong — on the job

caught up again
in a seemingly endless exhausting work year
made bearable only
by the prospect of another summer
on vacation

4

HERS . . . *His Moccasins*

I loved our family camp–outs
Except for the getting there
Ric driving through
Past the vistas   Past the view
Restaurants — restrooms
His bladder gaged with the gas tank
Never stopping for the children or me
His foot on the throttle
Making the kids pee in a bottle

Back then I never understood
Since there are certain things
Men are supposed to do
I naturally let ol' Dan'l Boone
Get mantles for the lantern
Buy white gas — lye for the john —   ice
Fishing licenses — hatchets — ropes — tents

One summer without him
The kids and I went   We loaded the car
Wrestling that puzzle into the trunk
The children packed the fishing tackle on top
To be the first to come out
As soon as we got there they grabbed it
And vanished wiley as trout
Leaving me to unpack
Gas up the lamp — dig the latrine
Put the watermelon and cans in the stream
Gather wood — fight the tent
Get hyperventilated on the air mattress
When i got through
Dizzy doing what he would have done
I could see why he said:

> *"Camping wasn't all that much fun."*

HIS ... to choke

is when the story goes well
the one you dearly love to tell
the flock responding
as you bring them toward the finale
racing about
like a clever boarder collie

but this evening
there is something in the wind
a crumb
a trace of wheat thin
something sucked in

.(*)

to lodge between the verb
and synonym
    and
    the silence that follows
    is not golden

and when neither wine or water
will touch it
helplessly you turn the story
over to your wife to finish
knowing
she never found it
particularly amusing

and also knowing
that while you sit there in tears
strangling
she will be getting
twice as many laughs as you would have
simply by mangling the punch line

        and that's what really
        sticks in your craw

HERS . . . *Permission*

Isn't it wonderful?
He let you do it.
Aren't you lucky?
He allowed you to do it.

I burned,
But I didn't call her on it.
I'd been there
I'd let him
Let me
> *for years*
> *and years*
> *and years*

HIS . . . and NOW

the women are organizing in the kitchen
they want a living wage for housework
and one of them
has it figured in such a way
the government would pay
which might be OK
until you consider coming home
at the end of a hard day
to find
        a teamster at the sink

HERS . . . *Lord Nelsen*

My husband always drives
But once down in Texas
On an empty road
Rolling along with the tumbleweed
He was tired enough
To let me take the wheel

The camper rocking in the wind
I was Lady Nelsen at the tiller
of a great sailing ship
When suddenly Lord Nelsen
Came to,
"Did you see that?
There was a tumbleweed
Fifty feet in the air.
Pull over — watch out
We'll be killed!
I'll drive."

"Act like a man, you baby,"
I said, the fun gone
As I pulled over.
He should be scared and miserable
At least half the time.
He'd been reading
The wind warning signs

"That's all"
                    he said.

HIS ... free at last

if she's part of the movement
she no longer wants to be a girl
    a chick
    or a broad
    not even a lady
she's a feminist
    a liberated woman
and i'm for this
a free female
means a free male
free enough to openly express
my childish insecurity

if a person
wants to whine and whimper
nowadays a person can
but everytime i do
my liberated woman
says
act like a man

HERS . . . *Housewife*

Jealousy and hate
That big bad wolf
Gobbled up my eyes
And a gruff Daddy voice
In my head
Continually said,
"It's not nice for women
To go out to work."

So I stayed in the house

No quiet, peaceful hilltop,
I was the faucet, an endless drip.
I cried, whined,
As I swept, mopped, ironed

I saw only the clothes, the outer man.
Got caught in the tie
Served my hands on a platter
Along with my head
To the man
"For the children's sake," I said.

But I let the house eat me.

HIS . . . tap roots

hunkered down back there in the half light
before the dawn when i couldn't see so good
looking out from under a shelf-like brow
i would watch her
      with the child
      with the life
      SHE
      had created

now this was before the word
and because i knew not the why of it
nor the how
i was filled with envy and rage
and i hated her
for try as i might
strain as i would
i the male
could create nothing more impressive
      than a turd

wasn't i bigger'n her and stronger
and so to cover my chagrin and disgrace
i gave her a cuff across the face
took up a spear
and walked out into the morning

be patient with me woman
i'm working on it
but when the tap root
goes down that deep into history
the tree is not easily moved

and now that you do have your sperm bank
and have mastered karate

      have i become irrelevant again?
      or just plain paranoid

HERS . . . A Woman's Place

Why do I long for another place
When I have my place,
This place where I can walk a
country road
With my dogs running up ahead,
Tune in on a bird's song,
Hear insect-rattle noises
See sky blues,
Clouds, trees, bushes,
Flower yellows,
Why do I long for another place
When I have this place, my place.
A woman's place.

HIS . . . coming & going

                    i have noticed
                    that men
                    somewhere around forty
                    tend to come in from the field
                    with a sigh
                    and removing their coat in the hall
                    call into the kitchen
                                            you were right
                                            grace
                                            it ain't out there
                                            just like you've always said

                    and she
                    with the children gone at last
                    breathless
                    puts her hat on her head
                                            the hell it ain't

                    coming and going
                    they pass
                    in the doorway

HERS . . . *Celebration*

I celebrate myself
The woman
The true woman
Not assumed
Not to be taken away
Billie Barbara
That is Billie Barbara
That is Billie Barbara
I am
An energy event!

HIS . . . telephone line

running beside the highway
the wires are alive with human souls
touching
and i at forty three
after the sunset again
drop
    a
      dime
and suddenly you
someone young
someone new
is there at the other end of the line
and i can feel myself
emptying into your presence

after the initial "hello"
you don't have to speak
it is enough
just listening to the space where you are
being together and alone at the same time
or talk about the weather
or what ever
it doesn't matter
when i know we are connected

and i can tell the difference
between dream and reality
and sometimes
out there in a glass box
they are the same

HERS . . . *Only the Now*

I can't go with you
After all there's the kids
And it was you, you were the one
Who always said;
"Only the now
That's all there is."
And When I did go along
I was the old shoe
comfortable forgotten
You were the closed door —

The elevator always somewhere else
On another floor.

HIS ... an impossible affair

to see a length of time through
to its conclusion
with someone close
can be a ripping business
for the end is always in sight
approaching relentlessly
the clock a death head
ever present — grinning
            a sure winner

from the start the action and cloing lines
                        memorized
me tearing myself
from the grip of your eyes
stumbling off stage blind and bleeding
clinging to dreams of brave gypsy children
riding the crest of the wind whipped now
singing
        i am alive
        and i know it

but what i have is mine
and even death
clever as he is
cannot take it from me

it was an impossible affair
and that
was exactly what i loved about it

HERS . . . No Blame

My house was dark
Alone — I ran out of dreams
Fell off the mountain,
Flew away over cities,
Had an affair
The quartered moon — poker-red
Burned into the darker depths,
Beyond the Blame.

On this side of sleep
I lie down on my fuzzy white coat
Reading Castaneda
Until the fog filling the canyon looks green.
If it were water
I could swim to another place,
I need to see things differently.
I can't be you, Mama,
Drowning in the berry patch
In the middle years.

Something is dying
Let me out!

HIS . . . mr. centerfold

a self-righteous
pseudo-perceptive woman once told me
that there had never been
a middle-aged man
who had gone to the trouble of losing
a great deal of over-weight
who
at the same time
wasn't having a secret affair

     or planning to

if you don't believe me
she said
just watch mr. centerfold on parade
marching sideways
to the bathroom mirror

a sweeping statement like that
is the thing in this world
i hate most of all
except perhaps
knowing that i have been nailed to the wall

HERS . . . *Color Me Blue*

This morning
My back hurts
Under my eyes — bags
My skin wrinkles — sags
There's no sun
The buildings are cold grey stones
Last night I dreamed of dying
Color me blue
I'm forty-two

HIS . . . a suicide attempt

a story always loses something
in the second telling
and so
            over the years he and she
developed a relationship
that needed a third party around
to break the silence
            when the children behaved
            the job secure
            if no one had died
            and the car didn't knock
they lived with the sound of the traffic outside
and the clock

            she survived
with the jr. league and a brownie troop
and when the kids grew up she went into group
            he held on playing golf
till his back wouldn't let him
then feeling his age one day
left home and flew to cleveland on business
checking into a motel
as a mr. and mrs. smith
but like the sales pitch says
            after one night in a holiday inn
            you'll not be surprised in the next

in retrospect i think the whole affair
was a kind of suicide attempt
on something gone humdrum
and he going to sleep that night
vaguely wondered
if the maid would arrive in time to turn off the gas
            if she did
            perhaps it would be a good omen
if not —
well a story always loses something
in the second telling

HERS . . . I Can Dance

(Dedicated to the critical parent tapes
that keep me like Hansel and Gretal
caged, waiting)

I awake Anne Sexton's child
Suicide's daughter
A cult with no hands
Cut off at the wrist
Without meaningful work
A displaced person, Anne Frank
A jew out of time
I would be Jane Eyre, the orphan
But I
> *Am*
> *My*
> *Own*
> *Punishing*
> *Parent*

Dizzy green nausea
Thick grey drips
Going round
I lie with the sun
Hidden under covers
No longer able to fix
My eyes spin in the browns
I have no center
My arms and legs
Spastic, jump on their own
I dance out of control
> *Watch me mama*
> *Down here*
> *In the pit with the snakes*
> *Watch me rock – Watch me roll*

HIS . . . waiting

i have in my life
stepped out on my wife
and tried waiting
in a white room
      for a young working woman
to bring me color
      through a white door

it has been a long morning
with this blank piece of paper
and quiet guitar
the sun came crawling on the floor
and i watched it with no more on my mind
than you
      and this slow

            unwinding
            lonely time

you will come soon for lunch
i will hear your sound in the hall
      your hand on the latch
and then time will fly
      till you're off to work again
      and i am left alone again
washing the afternoon walls
with my eyes
my god
to be a housewife waiting
      always waiting

           and you
           can't create
           while waiting
           you can only
               wait

HERS ... Waiting

And I have waited
I waited to grow up — use lipstick,
To be kissed, to wear a bra, for my prince
to come, to vote.
I waited for some man to ask me to marry him
and have children,
I waited in lines for stamps and groceries
In lobbies for movies
In parked cars for children at lessons
For airplanes to come bringing you in
For airplanes to go taking you out
I waited for the roast to get done, the jello
to set, the light to turn green,
Waiting to move on, to go away on vacations
and to go back home — the children grew up
And my hair is turning grey
And I have waited
For you to ask me to speak
for myself.
Hey! It's my turn. I will speak for myself.

HIS . . . the wedding dirdge

the good friday side of life
is where we find each other
touch each other
and realize
we are not alone alone

not at the christmas party
or easter picnic
true
these are good times
where joy has stopped the clock
dancing days
not to be overlooked

but remember this
       more of us are seen
       crying at a marriage ceremony
       than at a funeral service
       recognizing the sad fact
       i think
       that at the wedding we realize
       we could be
       in the presence of two free spirits
dying

The Contract

the set up

the nesting marriage over
the youngest bird ready to fly
both my wife billie barbara and i
after twenty years of fidelity
amazingly within 11 days of each other
and unbeknown to each other
broke the vows
she with an artist while i was on the road
and i with a young career woman in the midwest

the comical night i came home
and it all came to light
found us unable to be angry with each other
i mean
how can you get mad at someone
for doing the same thing you've been doing
(you can)
so we sat on the edge of the bed comparing notes
laughing
and wondering where our own relationship
had gone sour

from my male point of view
the only guilt i really had
was over the fact that at long last
i finally understood what billie had wanted
all those years she asked
for my full attention
i'd thought she'd had it
until i saw myself unable to pass a phone booth
without rushing in and dialing a chicago number
and buying silly dimestore gifts
to be delivered as i flew through o'hare airport

billie barbara in the meantime
out to dinner with her new gentleman friend
experiencing the kind of closeness
that can happen when a devoted lover
cuts the choice piece of meat from the center

of his steak
putting it on her plate
something she had not received from me
in twenty years of marriage

and i learned much about time
during this brief interlude
for being involved deeply with the young woman
and knowing the plane would fly in the morning
had me making the most
out of every stolen moment
and like a terminal cancer patient
knowing he had but a few months to live
i began to look up and see the sunset again
but then every human relationship
that has ever been or will ever be
ends
and i really began to get a grip on this fact of life

i had become the maintenance man to billie barbara
and she the big nurse to me
but talking through that night we realized
that there was an undeniable closeness between us
resting on things like waiting in hospital halls
to learn whether our son would die
after the motorcycle wreck
and yet our new loves had filled us with a zest
that we had lost somewhere in the maze
of everyday living

but rather than live together as dead people
or kick it all in the head and split
we decided to see if we couldn't find another alternative
to see if we couldn't put some sunsets
back into our own relationship

the following is our attempt
hammered out of our own lifestyle and personal needs
we do not think of it as an open marriage contract
rather creative divorce
or perhaps a better description would be
        beyond divorce

THE MASTENS' ANNUAL RELATIONSHIP RENEWAL

We, Richard and Billie Barbara, are terminating our legal marriage in divorce,[1BB] as we no longer believe in the state of wedlock. One human being cannot possess another; one human being cannot belong to another. Billie Barbara is no longer MY wife, Richard is no longer MY husband, henceforth the word "my" will be used to express relationship to, not possession of.[1r]

Realizing now, that intimacy[2BB] withers and dies in the face
—

[1BB] *After writing our contract, Ric and I were so excited. Holding hands we went to the Monterey County Courthouse and got the papers to file for a do-it-yourself divorce.*

Although it's no fault, the papers still read petitioner and respondent. As grounds for divorce we put infidelity and mental cruelty.

When we returned the papers, the clerk swelled up like a Bantie hen protecting her chicks, said, "You can't do this! Mr. Masten, Mrs. Masten, California is one of seventeen states where the only grounds for divorce are irreconcilable differences."

We went to a lawyer. He said go to Mexico or lie.
That was the point as far as we were concerned No More Lies!
We are not legally divorced. I began to realize what I wanted was a psychological divorce. Who am I, separate from Ric and the children?

[1r] I would never have admitted it then, but for the first 20 years of our relationship I considered Billie Barbara my personal property. I courted her, won her, and then with the help of church and state took her off the open market and made her mine. "Look folks, here comes my wife through my front door with my golf bag." Or at a party when she would be having a marvelous time with ol' Fred out in the kitchen, I'd find myself charging between them like an enraged bullmoose: "Billie, you're getting drunk, we're going home!"

[2BB] *Intimacy was a word like marriage I had never bothered to define. I thought we had one because we engaged in sex. Intimacy implies risk. I expose, offer myself. I can be straight with my feelings. I can ask to be listened to, to be held. I can throw a tantrum and know you won't feel responsibility for my behavior unless you are. I can ask you not to tell me what to do. I can ask you to encourage me to find my own answers, solutions. I can ask for your advice. I know you can reject me, hurt me. I still feel safe enough to risk it.*

of the phrase: "Till death do us part" which is not eternity, we are now willing to pay the price for that intimacy by giving up and letting go of false security.2r We have come to believe that the flower is only beautiful because we know its beauty will fade, and have found that a flower held to closely dies even more swiftly.3r

We enter now into a new relationship. One cycle. One year. One spring, where things start to bloom but are not fully realized. One summer, warm and lovely but also miserably hot. One autumn, beautiful but at times with chill in the air, and a winter that can be close and comfortable but also cold and freezing. We pledge to see one entire cycle year through, together, one year from this date *Sept. 3rd,* 4r and at the end of 365 days we will then decide whether we shall renew this relationship for another cycle year.

During the year when we are together, we will give each other our attention, time and thoughtfulness.3BB We will

—

2r   As I see it a marriage license was not designed simply to permit marriage. Rather it was conceived to give the little woman legal protection against her rascal of a husband during the expected eventual divorce proceedings, a document created by men to force some security for women in a male chauvenist society. God knows we didn't want them competing with us out there on the work force.

3r   Why are we offended when we discover the flowers in the restaurant are plastic? Perhaps because they've fooled us, but more than that I think it's because plastic flowers are intended to last forever. We bring cut flowers into our lives to keep us in touch with the "now;" we give them our immediate attention for we know they'll soon fade and be gone. Billie Barbara and I have come to believe that "Till death do us part" does not mean the relationship will last forever. Quite the contrary, it means death is going to part us, either a personal death or the death of the relationship. The bouquet must be enjoyed, in fact can only be enjoyed, *today.*

4r   In a separate legal document, I have guaranteed Billie Barbara an all-expense paid college education if she or I should ever decide not to continue our relationship. I consider this a form of retroactive pay for services rendered while I was out tooling up a career, 20 years of dishes and diapers while I became a successful poet and songwriter. And gentlemen, you'd be surprised how you start to bring flowers home again when you live with an option that might not be picked up next year.

3BB When I first married Ric, I cried if I didn't get to sit by him in the movies. He always saw something different from what I saw. I'd

32

respect each other's dignity and privacy and not expect
more than the other is willing to give. We will not use
honesty as brutality, 5r but will answer a question honestly
when asked, yet not tell more than the other wants to
know.4BB In short, we will respect each other's right to own
his or her own mind, body and spirit.5BB

We enter into this relationship knowing full well either one
—

*miss all those pearls. He was the most interesting person I knew.
Twenty years later, he was the last person I wanted to sit beside.*

*Ric, the person I loved the most, became the person I treated with
the least amount of common courtesy.*

5r   Before I found out that Billie Barbara was also "slippin' round"I hadn't
planned to tell her about what I was up to for any number of reasons, not
the least of which was that I didn't want to give her license to do what I was
doing. My secret had me troubled tho, because I knew myself well enough
to know I'd use it on her the next time we'd stage one of our bickering
sessions. Those midnight to morning screamers where Billie could show off
her remarkable ability to recall every mistake I'd ever made, waiting of
course, till 2 AM on a morning I had an early plane to catch before coming
up in the bed like the kid in the *Exorcist* with evil in her eye: "I want to talk!"
And she'd come on with "Remember 17 years, 4 months, 3 weeks, 2 days, 8
hours and 12 minutes ago when you went off to have a beer with Fred and
left me standing in the rain? Really caring person aren't you? And do you
remember . . ." and on and on like this while I, back to the wall, tried
desperately to remember even one thing she'd done wrong, something I
could never seem to do. The scene always ended at dawn with me raping
her and staggering off to the airport leaving her sleeping, an angelic smile on
her face. But now, suddenly, there was a new ingredient involved, a
devastating secret weapon in my arsenal, and I was certain I'd never play
our little game again to the traditional conclusion. The next time I knew I'd
fight back: "Well honey, you're right I am a SOB, and there's something else
I've been meaning to tell you — I have a mistress!" And wham! The winner
and new champion of the world. Look out for honesty. It can be a form of
brutality.

4BB When we wrote the contract we were both involved in other
    relationships. Ric told me he couldn't remember feeling for me
    what he felt for the other person. I felt hurt and cheated. We wrote
    this line to protect hurt feelings. Since then we've never used it in
    just this way as we are no longer involved in outside sexual
    relations.

5BB How can you love me and not believe the way I do? Yet I married
    him knowing he was an atheist and I was a fundamentalist.
    Naturally, since I had the truth I'd convert him to my way of
    thinking. He was thinking he could talk me out of mine.

33

of us might wish to terminate it at any time, and realizing that there will be moments of fear, anger and jealousy, we pledge to see each other through these times and only break this agreement when it is clear that it is a matter of absolute personal survival. This would be determined after counseling with a trained uninvolved third party (counselor, minister, etc.).

The reason we feel we want to enter into this relationship is because of history[6BB] and time spent together, and although our past relationship died we want to see if from that death something new can arise. The past has not been wasted and it will always be ours and we shall honor it as we do the fruit of that relationship, our children. We will never sever the past though we may wish to form new relationships. And the fact that we might not wish to renew this agreement does not mean that anything we have had is lost, but rather that two people moving forward in love have moved apart.[7BB]

6BB *During the crisis period when things were hardest I remembered only the bad times the things, I didn't like. Looking through photograph albums of our family, I was reminded that we'd had as much fun as tears. As Ric says, take a picture of everything, you'll need it later. I began to remember Ric as I first knew him. I realized many of the things that I hated about him were the very things that had drawn me to him in the first place. I had been attracted to his ways that were different from my ways.*

7BB *I was raised by a mother whose parents were divorced when she was fourteen, in a little Texas town where no one got divorced. So divorce was a very bad thing. Feeling so dependent on Ric, I needed to know independence. Ric and I decided to take a month when he was away and pretend the other were dead. It was during this time that I began to realize I was a survivor. All my life when things got bad I'd screamed suicide. I realized I wanted to live and it was a matter of becoming my own mother developing a nurturing parent inside my head, giving myself permission to experiment to see what I wanted to do. I needed to feel I had a choice in choosing an interdependent relationship. I had never been independent financially. Although I'm still not, I do make some of the income. I now have confidence in myself that if something happened to Ric I could support myself. I no longer feel that because I have unequal money power that I have no voice, no choice over my own life.*

Each year this ceremony may be rejected, rewritten, added to or subtracted from. This is not a contract of probability, rather it is an opening of all possiblities.

All things are possible now.6r

*

6r   What we have shared with you is not important in and of itself. The essence of all this is the fact that two people with a dead relationship sat down together and did something about it. Robert Frost says,"When you want to do a 'think' on something, write about it." You might say creative writing saved our marriage. Of course you can't put the glue that holds a relationship together into words, but Billie Barbara and I rediscovered what we had lost between the lines; however we needed to write the lines to have something to look between. What all of us are really after cannot be put on paper and this has always been the poet's dilemna. So, after Billie Barbara and I had made it through all of the above I wrote a little song for her. In it I try to explain why, in 20 years, I'd never written a poem or song for her before, sort of killing two birds with one stone. It ends this way —

> . . . . have i told you i love you?
> well how could I say it?
> with couplets and verses i'd never convey it
> words may be pretty as beads on a string
> but words are just words
> would you settle for the real thing?

Beyond Divorce

HIS . . . icarus

remembering what happened to icarus
i used to be uneasy in the air
flying with these damn wax wings of mine.
but since i have come through
a particularly wild flight
and seen how much pounding the ship can take
i hardly look up from my magazine these days
in the air pockets

i think that all too often we panic
at the height of the storm
and are too quick to cut the ropes
and throw everything overboard
and later in the doldrums
realize that perhaps we might have made it through
with everything intact.

i wonder if the ocean floor is not littered
literally littered
with the bones of those who abandoned ship
too soon

or
are you really
that much happier
since your separation?

HERS . . . *Ivory Soap*

I have in my life

D
R
O
P
P
E
D

Like a rock
Like a bar of soap
To the bottom

At 45
Not entirely
Ninety-nine one hundredth percent pure

I
Can
Still F   L   O   A   T

HIS . . . the quality of love

in the throes of the affair
i was surprised to learn
i could love two women
with intensity
at the same time
one with whom i'd spent many years
and one recently met

now
the quality of these loves
is best described by the difference
in my bathroom behavior — toilet procedure
        at home
though the room was occupied
(my wife in the tub)
when you gotta go
ya gotta go — and i always went
        but in an apartment near chicago
i would carefully close the door
run the water
and turn the fan on

during this time
if a doctor had informed me
i had but six months to live
looking back
i think
i would have chosen
        the apartment
for the first three months
but i know now
i would have wished to go home
to die
        with someone who knows just
        how full of crap
        i really am

HERS . . . *No Fear of Flying (A Dream)*

There were two of him
Gemini brothers, Siamese twins,

The little bearded man jumped ahead
An oddity, antsy
A see-through man
Papier-mache without the paper
All wired and dancy

The strong quiet man covered his head
Walked with me
Held me to him tightly
I could not see his face
But he kissed me with his tongue
We made love together nightly

We three walk a handmade road
A paved bridge with a hole to fall through
A view seen from a ridge

I had no fear of falling or flying

HIS . . . no strings

kites are one thing
but i have noticed the birds
            have no strings
and whether it is true or not
            doesn't matter
but i have looked upon you
as a wounded sparrow
            to be lifted
            and cupped in my hand
careful not to touch your broken wing

and there were times you pecked me
viciously
over things i could not fathom
but then god knows what a sorry sight
i made
bending over you
            in such concerned pity
so i left the cage

            open

hoping you'd be off

and suddenly it comes to my attention
how the front door
has been carefully left ajar

i notice this
as the morning sun is pouring
            across the floor
and if either of us should fly
            without a song

            it will all have been
            for nothing

HERS . . . *Again*

And he stood solid
Letting the sharp
Word edges bounce off and
Fall away —
Until we could come together —
Again and touch

THEIRS . . . The Warty Frog

once upon a time
a warty frog
had a princess come along
and kiss it
    nothing happened

but when another frog
hopped up
    something did

and for those of you
wondering what to do
while waiting
for your prince to come
i say
    enjoy the frog

The Talk Back

After presenting this material over the last five years, it made no difference whether we were in New York, Florida, Kansas, Minnesota, New Mexico or California. The questions asked in response to this presentation were essentially the same.

1. WHY DO YOU PUT YOUR WHOLE RELATIONSHIP ON DISPLAY, WHY DON'T YOU KEEP IT CONFIDENTIAL?

> *To give permission to others to get things out, talk about what's bothering them.*
> *To talk, or to tell anyone I had a problem was to admit I was a failure, so I kept things inside making myself sick.*
> *I need recognition. Trying to be Ric, negating parts of myself, I kept myself from finding my work, my poems, my creativity. It's my art, sharing what I see. Listening to you in response moves me toward understanding and empathy. Sharing helps me to think, to feel, to care, to be wonder-full.*

Many of these questions bring a poem to mind. Where I can I'll let the poem speak for me. As for this first question, lived experience has always been the grist for my poetic mill. But more than that, the kind of therapy that helps me most is *therapy in the field.*

> i wanted to thank you for taking the time
> to walk and talk with me this morning
> i can't begin to tell you
> how much it helped
>
> that's OK
> i was glad to do it
> however
> i thought that you
> were walking and talking with me

2. WHAT HAS REALLY CHANGED IN YOUR RELATION-SHIP?

My attitude. I no longer feel I should be, or I have to be, married. I'm in a relationship with Ric because I want to be. I went into marriage with my parents' — yesterday's definition, which I never bothered to think through or verbalize even with Ric. Now instead of two people trying to become one, our marriage relationship consists of two separate individual people, not born equal. Our talents, strengths, weaknesses, personalities, economic backgrounds, conditioning, etc. are different. We are one in will: we both value and want to keep our relationship. I no longer identify myself as just a wife, just a mother. Wifery and mothering are two things I can do. I am Billie Barbara.

For two or three years before our crisis period I had been encouraging Billie to get busy with herself, to get involved with things outside the house and family. She did. Later, embroiled in the affair, I happened to meet an old friend who had recently lost her husband to a beautiful young woman. After that conversation, I went home and did a "think" on it. The following is entitled *white water*.

> i
> who had just entered the rapids
> of estrangement
> was most interested in what she might say
> she
> who had just come through the white water
> the wild water
> the mad crazy part of the river
>
>> now tell me
>> for the past few years
>> have you encouraged

                    your dear spouse
                    to get with it and find herself
                    and be an entity unto herself?
        yes

                    and did she do it
                    i mean go out and find
                    something of value
                    aside from the house
                    the children and you?
        yes

                    now tell me
                    this strange young
                    unexplainable new object
                    of your affection
                    is she mostly a pool
                    for you to reflect upon?

        i hope there would be more to it than that
        but — well — yes

                    shit!
                    she said

From my point of view the most noticeable change in
my relationship with Billie Barbara is the fact that I now
find myself living with a strong capable individual, not
merely a devoted, untroubled (at least on the surface)
reflecting pool.

3. ISN'T ALL THIS UNNECESSARY, AS YOU ARE STILL LEGALLY MARRIED, AND WHY DO YOU THINK YOU NEED A WRITTEN CONTRACT?

Ric's willingness to sit down and talk with me, to listen to me as a person with interesting ideas helped me to reevaluate myself and him.

> *When I thought of myself as a failure*
> *That there was something wrong with me*
> *I thought there had to be something wrong with you*
> *For loving me.*

To share in the writing of our contract is necessary for me as I need to feel important that my ideas are valued by Ric. Talking had always been one of our problems. "I" statements have improved our communication. "You make me ..." always hooks into Ric's defensiveness and implies that he is responsible for my feelings. Planning how he could defend himself, "What did I do?", kept him from hearing me.
"I feel angry" doesn't imply he's responsible. His usual response to this is, "Do you want to talk about it?" Often just owning the feeling is enough: I feel better.
I like a written contract for reference and also as a reminder that Ric is someone I value.
A neighbor would come over, I'd say, "Hi, how are you? Sit down, let's talk. May I fix you a cup?"
Ric came home, not even a greeting. He'd go immediately into the living room, turn on the T.V. and start reading the newspaper. I'd go into the kitchen feeling hate, hurt, hate. I could hold onto these feelings all evening, yelling at the kids, then really letting go on Ric in bed, not able to tell him what it was all about. He though I was crazy.

About this time an old printer dropped by the print shop where Ric worked. He told the men if they wanted a happy marriage it would take one minute of their time each day and he guaranteed it would work. First thing you do when you get home from work, he told them, is take your wife into your arms, sweep her to the floor in a Valentino kiss, look her in the eye and say I love ya, honey!

We tried it and it worked. Now if Ric forgets to greet me I greet him. I used to think if Ric really loved me he'd know what I needed without me telling him. I would feel disappointed when he couldn't read my mind. Anyway it wasn't nice for a woman to ask to be loved, noticed.

Also, I feel more secure knowing when Ric goes off to work he'll come home.

The act of writing the document, of choosing words we both can live with put us back in touch with each other. Some have accused us of playing a foolish little word game. Perhaps we are, but who cares as long as it does the trick.

> . . . . sometimes i think we should play
>   ping pong
>   if the ball keeps coming back
>   across the net
>   at least we both know somebody's there
>   and that's what its all about anyway

4. WHAT HAPPENED TO THE "OTHERS?" TELL A LITTLE BIT MORE ABOUT THEM.

When I broke out of my marriage I was angry. I did it as an angry act, but I did it. No one made me, I chose to do it and if I ruined my life I did it, no more blame.

I wanted to be in control, I wanted to do what I thought men did — decide when we'd meet, have dates, where we'd go, etc. I remember saying to my new friend, "Teach me to be a man." This relationship didn't last long.

I then remembered another man I'd liked so I called him and asked to come see him. Staying with him helped me see him as just a bigger, older Ric.

Both these men were artists, both wanted a woman to play traditional wife roles, support them while they pursued their art. I'd done that once. What came through loud and clear was that I wanted to be supported while pursuing my career. I wanted to do art. I began to realize only Ric cared enough about me to help me do this. I went home. Never saw either one of them again. One is dead and I don't know what happened to the other one.

It was my morality that compounded the problem and had me making more of a one night stand than was probably necessary. I didn't like the feeling of having used another human being to masturbate with. So I was almost driven to do right by the young woman and free my wife from the "cheating bastard" she was married to. However, it is interesting to note that I chose a career woman to get involved with, someone who only had time and energy for a once-a-month lover. When it looked like it might be more than that she began to back pedal. As to what happened to her after we parted, I understand she did eventually get married to someone close to her own age.

5. DO YOU THINK YOU WOULD HAVE REACHED THIS PLACE HAD THERE BEEN NO "OTHERS", AND WHAT IF ONE OF YOU HAD HAD AN AFFAIR BUT THE OTHER HADN'T?

No, probably not. If Ric had had an affair and I hadn't, I already felt so bad about myself, had such a poor self image, I'd have used it as an excuse to go insane, commit suicide or get divorced.

In the early years I labored on a cement crew and after that spent some time in a print shop. The relationship seemed in good shape during this period, as I didn't particularly enjoy my work. Each evening Billie and I would sit down together and commiserate, she about the housework and I about my slave-driving boss. The moment I began to make a living doing what I enjoyed, presenting my songs and poetry, the domestic wheel began to wobble. My occupation became my lover, consuming me totally, and this was not an easy mistress for Billie to deal with. I mean, how can you complain about someone who writes a letter stating that a poem of mine caused them to call off an intended suicide attempt? Therefore I feel the "others" were an essential ingredient, a crisis that forced us to face problems that had always been there. The fact that we both had a secret affair at the same time was a miracle. If Billie had taken a lover and I hadn't, I'm not sure what I would have done. My guess is that I would have begun to take advantage of all those stage door Jeannies that had always been there, and I don't think I would have liked myself much for doing this.

6. WHAT IF YOU NEVER FELT FOR YOUR SPOUSE WHAT YOU ARE FEELING FOR THE "OTHER"?

No one asked me. What I learned was: I never felt with the "others" what I've felt with Ric. I wasn't aware until later that I never gave myself permission to feel love, to have orgasm during sex outside of marriage.

This question is never asked publicly. It comes in confidence, usually from a male, after our presentation. I understand the question, since during the involvement I told Billie Barbara much the same thing. It hurt her a great deal. Even now during our presentations it is still an area of pain and misunderstanding. The following is a poem I wrote for the young woman followed by a second look after the fires had been banked. I call it *the chicago fire*.

No one knows what goes on
behind the faces, for I live in your
golden shadow blinded by a rush of
bright madness, of burning morning
haze, and it is a wonder I function
at all.

Yet here in virginia I wander
down this quiet afternoon with
friends and clearly see the dogwood
exploding in a galaxy of gray
turning green. At my feet tiny
flowers, fern and moss are seen in
perfect detail.

Far from the midwest we walk at
the edge of spring, talking lightly
of things, voices in the trees, and no
one knows that i am being consumed
by the thought of you.

but now
in another space
        another place and time
i read the above
        curiously
like an old newspaper account
of the chicago fire
having no idea
of what it's really all about

like pain
such things
will not be remembered

7. IS YOUR RELATIONSHIP AN OPEN MARRIAGE SEXUALLY?

Yes

Up to now, however, neither one of us have exercised that option. The first tour I took alone after Billie Barbara and I had signed the contract put me in a college town where an attractive newspaper woman followed me around from class to class. Late that night after the concert I discovered she was still at my side. It was then that I realized she was there to interview me in depth. For the first time in my sexual life not only the opportunity, but also the option, were present at the same time. And what did I do? I backed away from the situation, not for the usual "because it is forbidden" reason, but because I had a heavy schedule of classes the next day starting with an 8 o'clock. What I did not need was a wild night of sexual gymnastics. What I needed was a good night's sleep. And anyway, if you can't say "no" your "yes" means nothing.

Over the years, Billie Barbara and I have met many people involved in sexually open marriages and have watched most of them rattle apart. The breaking point seems to come the night someone feels the need to be with the person they consider primary only to find that, at that particular time, the primary is busy with somebody else. I doubt if anyone really wants to feel secondary to the one they consider primary.

8. DID THE RELATIONSHIP BETWEEN YOU AND YOUR CHILDREN CHANGE DURING ALL THIS, AND WHAT DO THEY THINK OF YOUR CONTRACT?

No, the kids were supportive of both of us.
They knew we were going through a hard time.
They now say Mom and Dad are happily married again.
When our oldest daughter married she didn't write her own contract, she married traditionally forever. Our children think that contracting is fine for us but they'll find their own way.

When my daughter Ellen came along, she being the youngest of four, all the parts were taken except "negative." She and I had a standoff relationship right from the start. When it looked like Billie and I might separate, she let us both know that she wanted only me as her daddy, and we became closer than we'd ever been before. Also during this period another interesting thing happened having to do with my mother and I. As a young woman she'd been involved in a notorious affair that was the talk of the town, and I'd never forgiven her for doing this to my father. At long last the righteous child understood, and more than that, began to realize how much alike *mother and son* really are.

> there have been two creatures on this earth
> i could never get the best of
> my dog
> and my mother
>
> whenever i would catch either one of them
> up to no good
>   chewing a shoe
>   or sneaking through a drawer
> one would become deathly ill
> the other
> pee on the floor

the dog is gone now
piddling around out there
beyond my kick and frustrated shout
and feeling a sudden chill today
i pulled on a sweater
at the sleeve
guess whose hand came out
      shaking a thermometer

9. WOULD YOU CONTRACT ONE YEAR AT A TIME IF YOU HAD SMALL CHILDREN?

No, I would contract but the contract would be different. With children who have been planned for, the time of their growing up would have to be considered in the contract.

The hope of the world is parents who plan for children, where every child is wanted, brought into the world by conscious choice.

Perhaps we could divide a lifetime relationship into four seasons.

Springtime (the learning years) would be when a young couple might commit themselves a year at a time, giving themselves a chance to find out if they can squeeze a toothpaste tube together, letting themselves discover that even the most wonderful person farts in bed. This period would be used to experience things never considered in a traditional courtship.

Summertime (the building years) arrives when the two people who have been living together make a conscious choice to have a child, now quite possible, contraception being what it is. With this important decision, I think the deadline should be extended to the day that the youngest child graduates from high school. This built-in deadline might reduce the surprise for the female when the period of active mothering is over.

Autumn (the maintenance years) back to contracting a year at a time, as Billie Barbara and I are doing, trying to keep the relationship from falling into the "cricket lighter" syndrome — get one, use it up, throw it out. Up to this point our whole culture has been a springtime, summertime thing, with no sense of maintenance, of learning how to keep the wheels running smoothly.

Winter — well, being only 48 I can only speculate on what to call these years. Right now I have the feeling that

59

literal death is close enough that you don't need to create a deadline with a piece of paper. I must tell you here of an elderly man who spoke up during one of our presentations saying, "Mr. Masten, I don't take kindly to your 'wintertime' concept. I'm 86 years old and what makes you think I can't still get it up?" His remark brought the house down. The very next night I told that story to another group and when I did a gray-haired woman shouted from the back of the hall, "I want the name of that old gentleman!"

10. HAVE YOU CHANGED THE CONTRACT ANY SINCE YOU WROTE IT?

No, it's still working. The most challenging part of revolution is evolution . . . putting to work in our lives the new possibilities we're aware of.

For the past five years on each September 3rd we have ratified the original agreement, and we have ended every celebration singing *let it be a dance* with friends and family. The lyrics might be an appropriate note on which to end this odyssey.

let it be a dance we do
may i have this dance with you
through the good times
and the bad times too
let it be a dance

let a dancing song be heard
play the music say the words
and fill the sky with sailing birds
and let it be a dance
learn to follow learn to lead
feel the rhythm fill the need
to reap the harvest plant the seed
and let it be a dance

everybody turn and spin
let your body learn to bend
and like a willow with the wind
let it be a dance
a child is born the old must die
a time for joy a time to cry
take it as it passes by
and let it be a dance

the morning star comes out at night
without the dark there can be no light
and if nothing's wrong then nothing's right
so let it be a dance

let the sun shine let it rain
share the laughter bear the pain
and round and round we go again
so let it be a dance

let it be a dance we do
may i have this dance with you
through the good times
and the bad times too
let it be a dance